Dedicated to our children:

Yonah, who makes music,

and Daniel, who makes bread

—D. G. and P. G.

To my parents

—E. S. S.

Henry Holt and Company, LLC / *Publishers since 1866*
115 West 18th Street / New York, New York 10011

Henry Holt is a registered
trademark of Henry Holt and Company, LLC

Text copyright © 1995 by David and Phillis Gershator
Illustrations copyright © 1995 by Emma Shaw-Smith
All rights reserved.
Distributed in Canada by
H. B. Fenn and Company Ltd.

Library of Congress Cataloging-in-Publication Data
Gershator, David. Bread is for eating / David and Phillis Gershator;
illustrated by Emma Shaw-Smith.
Text in English; song lyrics in English and Spanish.
Summary: Mamita explains how bread is created in a
song sung in both English and Spanish.
[1. Bread—Fiction. 2. Songs—Fiction. 3. Hispanic Americans—Fiction.]
I. Gershator, Phillis. II. Shaw-Smith, Emma, ill. III. Title.
PZ7.G314Br 1995 [E]—dc20 91-28811

First published in hardcover in 1995 by Henry Holt and Company
First Owlet paperback edition, 1998
Printed in the United States of America on acid-free paper. ∞

ISBN 0-8050-3173-1 (hardcover)
3 5 7 9 10 8 6 4 2
ISBN 0-8050-5798-6 (paperback)
3 5 7 9 10 8 6 4 2

The artist used inks on Strathmore bristol to create the illustrations for this book.

David and Phillis Gershator

BREAD

IS FOR

EATING

illustrated by Emma Shaw-Smith

Henry Holt and Company • New York

"**B**read is for eating," Mamita says when I
leave bread on my plate. "Bread is for eating!"
And she sings this song to me:
> "El pan es para comer
> El pan es para la vida
> No tires el pan!
> Ay, ay! Vida mía."

"Think of the seed, asleep in the ground.

Think of the earth, a dark, cozy bed."

"Think of the sun, shining down on the earth.

Think of the rain, waking the seed from its slumber."

"I'm thinking, Mamita. I'm thinking about the little sprouts coming up from the ground."

And Mamita says, "This song is for the sprouting seed:

"El pan es para comer
El pan es para la vida
No tires el pan!
Ay, ay! Vida mía."

"Think of the farmer, who tills the soil, hoping
the rains will come on time.
Think of the harvester, who cuts the wheat and
catches the grain."

"Is it time for a song—a song for the grains of wheat?"
"El pan es para comer
El pan es para la vida
No tires el pan!
Ay, ay! Vida mía."

"Think of the worker, who loads the grain and
takes it to town.

Think of the miller, who grinds grain into
   flour, so soft and fine.
Think of the storekeeper, who sells us the flour."

"Yes, I'm thinking, Mamita. I'm thinking about the money we need to buy flour."

And Mamita says, "This song is also for the families working all day to put bread on the table:

"*El pan es para comer*
El pan es para la vida
No tires el pan!
Ay, ay! Vida mía."

"Think of the cook, kneading flour with water and yeast.

Think of the baker, baking bread before dawn."

"Think of the people around the world, dreaming of bread."

"I'm hungry for bread, Mamita," I say. "Then toast it and butter it or spread it with jam. Eat it cold, eat it hot. Eat a little, eat a lot. *¡El pan es bueno!*"

"We thank the seed, earth, sun, and rain for the grain, the beautiful grain, and sing for the bread that gives us life again and again and again."

"Will you sing the song with me?"
"El pan es para comer
El pan es para la vida
No tires el pan!
Ay, ay! Vida mía."

Bread Is for Eating

El pan es para comer

Words and music by David Gershator
Arranged by Yonah Gershator

Latin feeling—moderate tempo

mf *El pan es para co - mer.* *El*
— Bread is so good to eat. —

pan es pa - ra la vi - da. ¡No ti - res el
Bread is the staff of life. — Don't throw the bread a -

pan! *¡Ay, ay! Vi - da mí - a.*
way! Ay, ay! Love of my life.